# Flying Solo Viola

Unaccompanied

folk and fiddle fantasias

for playing your viola anywhere

Book Two

## Myanna Harvey

Front Cover Image: Science, Industry and Business Library: General Collection , The New York Public Library. "Estampe anglaise de 1843 représentant l'aèroplane d'Henson dans un vol supposé aux environs de Londres." The New York Public Library Digital Collections. 1922. https://digitalcollections.nypl.org/items/627e815a-d992-c1e5-e040-e00a18062370

A note about metronome markings: The tempo markings are suggestions only. These pieces may be learned and played at any tempo the player chooses. For the faster solos, there is no speed limit!

CHP404

www.charveypublications.com - print books
www.learnstrings.com - PDF downloadable books
www.harveystringarrangements.com - chamber music

# Flying Solo Viola, Book Two

### all tunes arranged by Myanna Harvey

## Table of Contents

# Flying Solo Viola, Book Two

## Haste to the Wedding

Trad., arr. M. Harvey

# Arirang

Trad., arr. M. Harvey

# Scarborough Fair

Trad., arr. M. Harvey

# Shenandoah

Trad., arr. M. Harvey

## Congress Reel

Trad., arr. M. Harvey

Flying Solo Viola, Book Two

11

©2022 C. Harvey Publications® All Rights Reserved.

# Mary Hamilton

Trad., arr. M. Harvey

# Lord Garrick

Trad., arr. M. Harvey

## Kerry Dancing

Trad., arr. M. Harvey

# Wild Mountain Thyme

Trad., arr. M. Harvey

# President Garfield

Trad., arr. M. Harvey

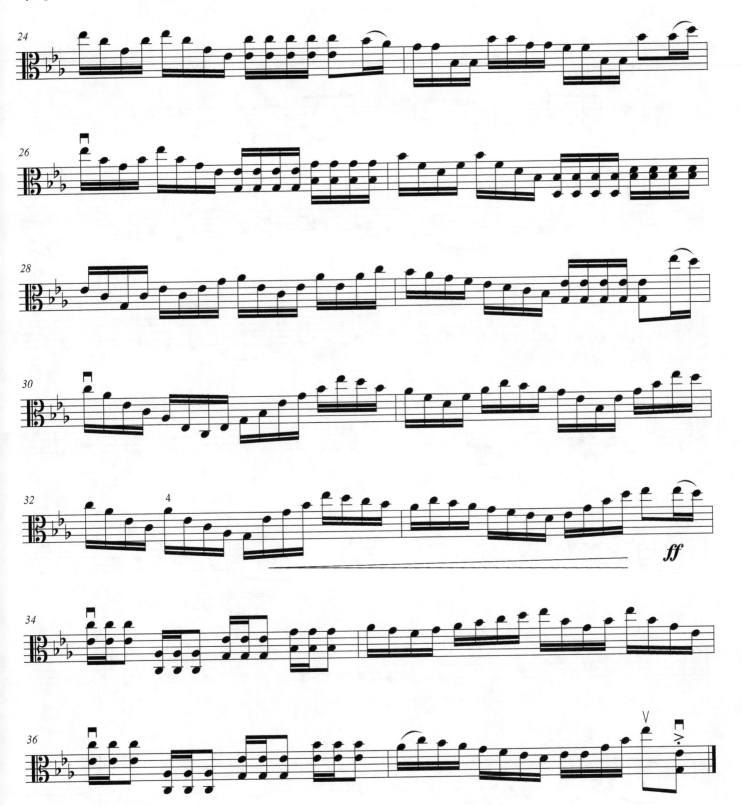

# Danny Boy

Trad., arr. M. Harvey

# Aiken Drum

Trad., arr. M. Harvey

## Salley Gardens

Trad., arr. M. Harvey

## Coleraine

♪ = 152-168

Trad., arr. M. Harvey

## After the Battle of Aughrim

Trad., arr. M. Harvey

# The Last Rose of Summer

Trad., arr. M. Harvey

♩= 96-120

# Roumanian Hora

Trad., arr. M. Harvey

## Waltzing Matilda

Trad., arr. M. Harvey

## Morrison's Jig

Trad., arr. M. Harvey

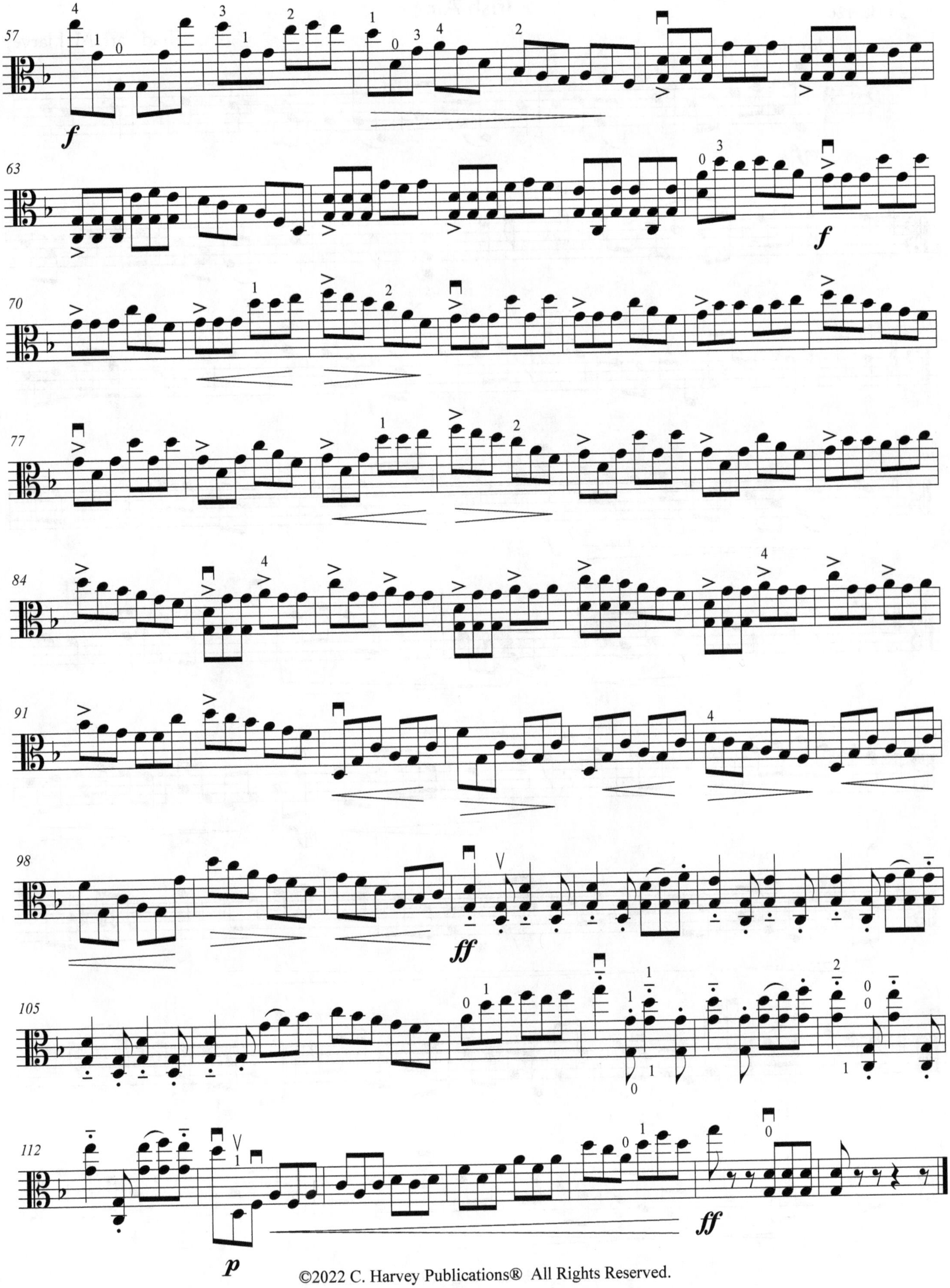

# Irish Air

Trad., arr. M. Harvey

# Peace Like a River

Trad., arr. M. Harvey

# Dark Eyes

**Freely, with Passion**

Hermann, arr. M. Harvey

# You Might Also Like:

## Fiddles on the Bandstand: Fun Duets for Two Violas
## Book One

all duets arranged by Myanna Harvey

### Table of Contents

CHP368
$9.95          www.charveypublications.com

Take a journey to a simpler time when lawn chairs and blankets would be out under the stars and music would waft out from under the eaves of the wooden bandstand.

These are the tunes that got our feet moving, made us smile, and brought us together. Now, with these viola duets, you can bring the toe-tapping, exuberant joy to others and remind us all that through highs and lows, music can be something we share to keep our spirits up and build community.

From Scott Joplin to John Philip Sousa, these viola duets will invite you up on the bandstand, out for a gig, or out on your lawn to play your heart out! Know any violinists or cellists? You can pick up a copy of the violin or cello book and play with those instruments as well; the viola book is fully compatible with the violin and cello books.

This viola book is in first and third positions and is at an intermediate level.